Aa Bb Cc Dd Ee Ff

Zz Gg

Yy Hh

Xx Ii

Ww Jj

Vv Kk

Uu Ll

Tt Mm

Ss Rr Qq Pp Oo Nn

Children's Picture Dictionary

written by Clare Humphreys

illustrated by Katy Sleight

Note to parents

This first picture dictionary is designed for children of three to seven years old. It includes over 190 key words arranged alphabetically and set in a large, easy-to-read text. Each word is explained by a picture and a short sentence.

Books are a very important part of a child's learning development and this picture dictionary introduces the child to letters of the alphabet and their order in an attractive and lively way.

Copyright © 1989 by World International Publishing Limited.
All rights reserved.
Published in Great Britain by World International Publishing Limited,
An Egmont Company, Egmont House, P.O. Box 111, Great Ducie Street,
Manchester M60 3BL.
Printed in Italy   ISBN 0 7235 2046 9
A CIP catalogue record for this book is available from the British Library

aeroplane

An **aeroplane** flies high in the sky.

alphabet

There are twenty-six letters in the **alphabet**.

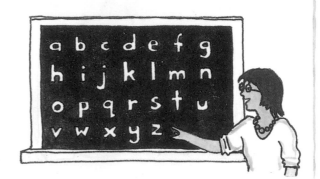

ambulance

An **ambulance** takes sick people to hospital.

animal

There are lots of kinds of **animals**.

ant

An **ant** is an insect.

apple

Apples grow on trees.

apron

An **apron** helps to keep us clean.

arm

Monkeys have long **arms**.

arrow

An **arrow** points the way.

astronaut

An **astronaut** travels in a spaceship.

Bb

ball
This **ball** bounces high.

banana
A **banana** is a fruit with a yellow skin.

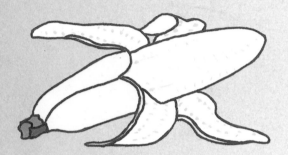

bed
We go to sleep in a **bed**.

bicycle
A **bicycle** has two wheels.

bird
A **bird** has wings and feathers.

boat

A **boat** sails on water.

boy

The **boy** plays with his puppy.

bucket

The **bucket** is full of water.

butterfly

A **butterfly** has four wings.

buttons

Buttons fasten our clothes.

Cc

carrot

A **carrot** is
a vegetable.

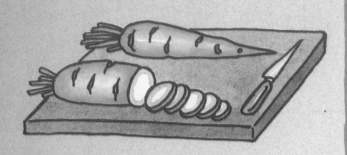

cat

The **cat** likes
drinking milk.

chair

A puppy sleeps
on the **chair**.

cheese

Cheese is made
from milk.

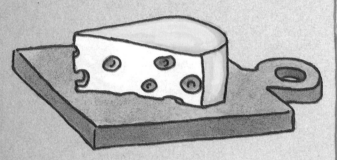

clock

A **clock** shows
us the time.

cloud

There are **clouds** in the sky.

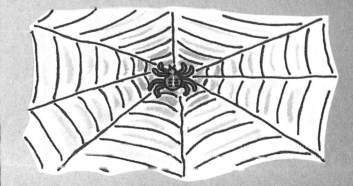

cobweb

A spider spins a **cobweb**.

cow

A **cow** gives us milk.

crown

The queen wears a **crown**.

cup

Here is a **cup** and saucer.

Dd

daisy

A **daisy** is a small flower.

dentist

A **dentist** looks after our teeth.

desk

We sit at a **desk** at school.

doctor

A **doctor** helps to make sick people better.

dog

A **dog** barks.

doll
The **doll** has a red skirt.

donkey
A **donkey** has long ears.

door
The **door** is open.

drink
We have a **drink** when we are thirsty.

duck
The **duck** is swimming.

Ee

eagle
An **eagle** is a large bird.

ear
We hear with our **ears**.

egg
Birds lay **eggs**.

elephant
An **elephant** has a long trunk.

emerald
An **emerald** is a green jewel.

Ee

engine
An **engine** makes a car go.

envelope
You post a letter in an **envelope**.

escalator
An **escalator** is a moving staircase.

exit
The **exit** is the way out.

eye
You see with your **eyes**.

Ff

farm

A **farm** has many animals.

fence

The cat is sitting on a **fence**.

fish

Fish live in water.

flag

The **flag** is blowing in the wind.

frog

The **frog** is sitting on a lily pad.

gate

The garden **gate**
is open.

giraffe

A **giraffe**
has a long neck.

glass

We can drink
out of a **glass**.

gloves

Gloves keep
your hands warm.

guitar

A **guitar** is a
musical instrument
that has strings.

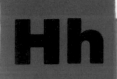

hair

This girl is brushing her long **hair**.

hamburger

A **hamburger** is a tasty, hot snack.

hammer

A **hammer** is a tool for hitting nails.

hand

The boy's **hands** are dirty.

hat

We wear **hats** on our heads.

hedgehog

A **hedgehog** has lots of prickly spines.

hen

The mother **hen** has four chicks.

hill

A **hill** is a small mountain.

horse

You can ride on a **horse**.

house

A **house** is a place to live.

igloo

An **igloo**
is a snow house.

ink

A pen writes
with **ink**.

insect

An **insect** has
six legs.

island

An **island** has
water all around it.

ivy

Ivy is a plant
that can grow
on walls.

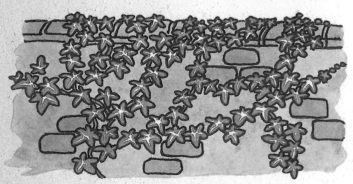

jar

This **jar** is full of jam.

jellyfish

A **jellyfish** has a nasty sting.

jewel

A diamond is a **jewel**.

jockey

A **jockey** rides races on a horse.

juice

We drink the **juice** that is squeezed from fruit.

kangaroo

A baby **kangaroo** sits in his mummy's warm pouch.

kennel

A **kennel** is a dog's house.

kettle

We boil water in a **kettle**.

key

This **key** unlocks the door.

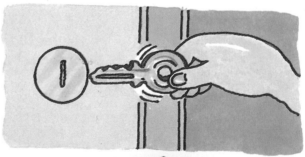

king

The **king** is sitting on his throne.

kitchen

The lady is cooking in the **kitchen**.

kite

A **kite** flies in the wind.

kitten

A **kitten** is a baby cat.

knife

We eat with a **knife** and fork.

knot

This is a **knot** in a rope.

ladder

We use a **ladder** to reach high places.

lamb

A **lamb** is a baby sheep.

lamp

A **lamp** gives us light.

leaf

This is an oak **leaf**.

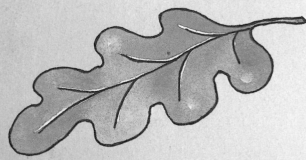

lemon

A **lemon** is a bitter, yellow fruit

letter

We write **letters** to our friends.

lettuce

Rabbits like to eat **lettuce**.

lightning

Lightning flashes across the sky.

lion

A **lion** has a shaggy mane.

lollipop

Lollipops are sweets on a stick.

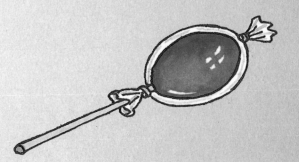

Mm

man

This **man** is very strong.

map

A **map** helps you to find the way.

mask

The girl wears a funny **mask**.

mirror

The kitten can see itself in the **mirror**.

money

We need **money** to buy things.

moon
We see the **moon** at night.

mop
We use a **mop** to clean the floor.

moth
A **moth** flies at night.

mouse
A **mouse** is a very small animal.

mushroom
Mushrooms are shaped like small umbrellas.

nail

A **nail** is used to join pieces of wood together.

necklace

I wear a **necklace** round my neck.

needle

You sew with a **needle** and thread.

nest

Birds build **nests** to lay their eggs in.

nettle

A **nettle** is a plant with stinging hairs.

newspaper

A **newspaper** tells us the news.

night

Stars come out at **night**.

nose

You smell things with your **nose**.

nurse

A **nurse** looks after you in hospital.

nut

Nuts are good to eat.

octopus

An **octopus** has eight legs.

onion

Peeling **onions** can make you cry.

orange

An **orange** is a juicy fruit.

orang-utan

An **orang-utan** is a type of monkey.

orchestra

An **orchestra** plays music.

organ

An **organ** is like
a piano with pipes.

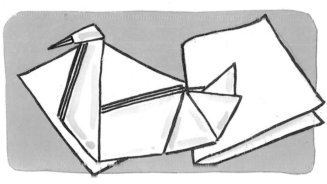

origami

Origami is folding
paper to make things.

ostrich

An **ostrich**
is a very big bird.

oven

We cook food
in an **oven**.

owl

An **owl** hunts
at night.

Pp

pencil
You can draw with a **pencil**.

piano
A **piano** is a musical instrument with lots of keys.

pineapple
Pineapples are large fruits.

pony
A **pony** is a small horse.

puppet
Puppets are fun to play with.

quarry
Rocks are dug out of a **quarry**.

quarter
This cake has been cut into four **quarters**.

queen
A **queen** lives in a palace.

question
We ask a **question** to find out something.

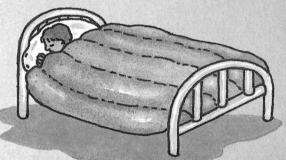

quilt
A **quilt** keeps you warm in bed.

rabbit

Wild **rabbits** dig
burrows to live in.

railway

A **railway** is a track
which trains run on.

rainbow

A **rainbow**
has seven colours.

ribbon

The parcel is tied
with a **ribbon**.

ring

I wear a **ring**
on my finger.

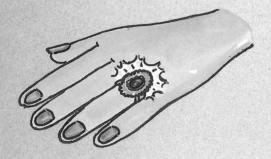

river
Boats sail on the **river**.

rocket
A **rocket** travels in space.

rope
Rope is like very thick string.

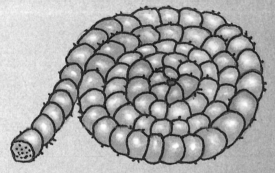

rose
A **rose** is a pretty flower.

ruler
We measure things with a **ruler**.

Ss

sandwich

A **sandwich** is made with bread.

scarf

A **scarf** keeps your neck warm on cold days.

seesaw

A **seesaw** goes up and down.

ship

A **ship** is a big boat.

shoes

We wear **shoes** on our feet.

shop
Things are sold
in a **shop**.

soap
Soap and water
makes you clean.

spade
I play with my bucket
and **spade**.

sun
The **sun** shines
in the sky.

swing
The girl plays on
the **swing**.

table

There is a vase
on the **table**.

tail

The squirrel
has a bushy **tail**.

tap

Water comes out
of a **tap**.

television

The boy is watching
television.

tent

You can go camping
in a **tent**.

tiger

A **tiger** is a large, wild cat.

towel

You dry yourself with a **towel**.

tractor

The farmer drives his **tractor** in the field.

tree

A **tree** has a trunk and leafy branches.

trousers

The clown is wearing funny **trousers**.

Uu

umbrella

An **umbrella** keeps us dry in the rain.

underwear

Underwear goes under our clothes.

unicorn

A **unicorn** is a fairytale horse.

unicycle

A **unicycle** has only one wheel.

uniform

Nurses and sailors wear **uniforms**.

van

A **van** is like a car for carrying things.

vase

You can put flowers in a **vase**.

vegetable

Vegetables are good for us to eat.

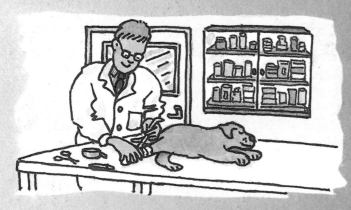

vet

A **vet** looks after sick animals.

violin

A **violin** is played with a bow.

Ww

wall

This **wall** is made of bricks.

whistle

You blow a **whistle** to make a noise.

window

A **window** lets light into buildings.

wizard

A **wizard** makes magic in fairy stories.

worm

A **worm** has no legs – it wriggles through the soil.

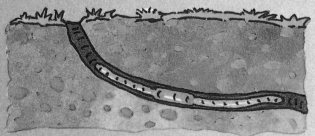

x-ray

An **x-ray** shows
us if any bones
are broken.

xylophone

The boy and the clown
are playing
xylophones.

yacht

A **yacht**
is a sailing boat.

yellow

Buttercup flowers
are **yellow**.

yogurt

Yogurt is
made from milk.

yolk

The **yolk**
is the yellow part
of an egg.

yo-yo

A **yo-yo** goes
up and down.

zebra
A **zebra** has
black and white stripes.

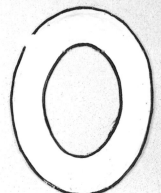

zero
Zero is the word
for the number 0.

zigzag
This is a
zigzag line.

zip
You can fasten
your clothes with
a **zip**.

zoo
We can see wild
animals in a **zoo**.

Aa	**Bb**	**Cc**	**Dd**	**Ee**	**Ff**
Zz					**Gg**
Yy					**Hh**
Xx					**Ii**
Ww					**Jj**
Vv					**Kk**
Uu					**Ll**
Tt					**Mm**
Ss	**Rr**	**Qq**	**Pp**	**Oo**	**Nn**